Biblical Economics: Financial Advice from the Book of Proverbs

February 2024

Written by Shanelle Shalom

Queens of Virtue Marriage Prep & Femininity Coaching

Introduction

FOR THE LOVE OF MONEY IS THE ROOT OF ALL EVIL. ~1 TIMOTHY 6:10

We've all heard people say, *"Money is the root of all evil,"* but a few very important words were left out of this quote. Money is *not* evil, and *having* money is not evil, but *loving* money can definitely lead us to do evil things. It's only right that we begin *Biblical Economics* by debunking the most common misconception about money among the body of Christ. The idea that money is evil or leads to evil outcomes causes us not to invest much thought into acquiring, managing, and multiplying our money.

Those of us who grew up in poverty are more inclined to have negative beliefs about money. When you're poor, it makes you feel better to believe that it's bad to have money because it gives you a sense of comfort. But even those who were never poor can still have a poverty (or scarcity) mindset. Although America is one of the most well-to-do countries on earth, the average American is living paycheck to paycheck. They're addicted to frivolous spending, they're up to their eyeballs in debt, and they do not have enough savings to carry them through the next six months if a crisis were to strike. They work extra hours and side hustles to make ends meet and aren't able to retire early, even if they wanted to. This is obviously not the lifestyle of people who are good with money. Although the average American is not "filthy rich," their financial habits are just as filthy as they believe the rich to be.

Let's face it, most of us aren't the best role models for how money should be managed. But that's okay, because the fact that you picked up *Biblical Economics* shows that you have an interest in learning about money from a healthy perspective. Oftentimes, people don't desire wealth for the right reasons, nor do they take the right steps to acquire it. They want to live the luxurious lifestyle that celebrities have—traveling, shopping, attending fancy events, and outings. And don't get me wrong, there is nothing wrong with these things, but they don't model the true purpose of money. **The purpose of money is to use it to build a lifestyle likened unto the kingdom of God.** As Matthew 6:10 says, *"Thy kingdom come. Thy will be done in earth, as it is in heaven."* The so-called "American Dream" has nothing to do with this mission, and that is why so many people of God fail trying to achieve and maintain it.

Striving to achieve the American Dream forces us to abide by the money laws of the world, which creates a scenario where a few live comfortably while everyone else lives life on a hamster wheel. We intuitively know that there is something wrong with an economic system that only seems to work for 10% of the nation. This is partially why so many people have such a negative view of money. If only a few are truly thriving financially while everyone else struggles, then it's difficult to view money as a positive. Good thing God has presented us with an alternative. We have a responsibility to extend God's kingdom, on earth as it is in heaven. We shouldn't try to recreate the lifestyle of the rich and famous because they are not building their lifestyles based upon scriptural instructions. They do what they want, and their decisions lead to a decline in their financial, physical, and mental wellbeing.

When we build our lifestyle likened unto the kingdom of God, we won't only have the same luxuries that the rich enjoy, but we'll also enjoy non-tangible riches such as peace and health. Money doesn't buy happiness, but living by *kingdom principles* definitely brings happiness to our lives. It just so happens that money is a benefit to living by these principles. As you read *Biblical Economics*, you will see that spiritual laws are a part of

God's economic system. You will also learn practical ways of building wealth that are frequently overlooked because they seem like common sense, even though they aren't commonly practiced. We think money is complicated, but it's actually pretty simple. Let me show you how simple it really is...

Biblical ECONOMICS

FINANCIAL ADVICE FROM THE BOOK OF PROVERBS

SHANELLE SHALOM

Ambition

WE ARE REMEMBERED FOR WHAT WE'VE DONE, NOT FOR WHAT WE SHOULD'VE DONE.

"He that is despised and hath a servant is better than he that honoreth himself and lacketh bread." ~Proverbs 12:9

Everyone can become complacent, no matter what their income is, but there is danger in being complacent in poverty. When you feel like you're already accomplished despite your financial instability, you will never strive to have more. This isn't to say that you should feel like a failure in your current situation, because you shouldn't. After all, we can't always control the factors that lead to financial instability. There are people who are born into impoverished conditions through no fault of their own. But you don't have to stay in the conditions you were born into, nor do you have to stay in the conditions that you created with bad financial decisions.

When you see someone who's in a better financial situation than yours, you are likely looking at someone who was *not* complacent in their conditions and did the work necessary to change them. Even though these well-off people may be envied by those who are less fortunate, the word of God says that it is better to be in their position than to be prideful, yet living in poverty. There isn't anything honorable about poverty. The honor is in striving for something better so that you and your family don't have to live each day struggling to get by. Lack puts strain on relationships and families, and we shouldn't be okay with our loved ones carrying this burden. You must get up, get out, and make something happen—something that will change your financial predicament forever. No longer settle for just getting by. We are not here simply to get by, but to achieve.

BETTER LATE THAN NEVER, BUT NEVER LATE IS BETTER.

"How long will thou sleep, O sluggard? When will thou arise out of thy sleep? Yet, a little sleep, a little slumber, a little folding of the hands to sleep. So shall thy poverty come as one that travelleth, and thy want as an armed man."
~Proverbs 6:9-11

We all procrastinate. While it may seem like an innocent habit, it can lead to serious problems if done frequent enough. Those who become the most successful in life are not big procrastinators. They get up earlier than most, put in more hours, and do it repeatedly until it becomes a habit. They accomplish way more in their day than the average person, and more often than not, it pays off. When we procrastinate, we make our day a lot less productive than it has to be. Instead of making the most of our day, we waste it away thinking, *"I can just do it later,"* and when later comes, we still don't want to do it. This level of procrastination eventually evolves into *laziness*, which can lead to failure in all areas, but especially financially. This doesn't mean that everyone who is struggling financially is lazy, but laziness will always lead to poverty and failure once it becomes a habit. We all have 24 hours in our day. How we use it makes all the difference. While some spend their 24 hours saying, *"I'll do it tomorrow,"* others wake up a few hours earlier so they can get it done *today.*

PLAY TIME IS OVER.

"For the drunkard and the glutton shall come to poverty, and drowsiness shall clothe a man with rags." ~Proverbs 23:21

You can usually tell if someone is going to be successful by how they spend their spare time. Some spend the majority of their spare time having fun or engaging in some activity that will hurt them more than it'll help them. It all seems harmless at first, but once they find themselves in physical, mental, and financial ruin, they see how destructive their habits are. We may not be drunks or gluttons like Proverbs 23:21 speaks of, but we all have other indulgences that can be just as destructive. Make no mistake about it, wealthy folks definitely have their fun too, but they exercise discipline in other areas, doing many of the things that others won't do or don't feel like doing, and this is what keeps them ahead of the pack.

There is nothing wrong with making time for leisure. In fact, it's actually a must that you do so. If you work hard, then it's only right that you have time to do something enjoyable for yourself. But you also should have enough discipline to know when play time is over and when play time isn't necessary at all. While building wealth, there *will* be times when you don't have time for leisure. You won't be able to go out for drinks, buy a new pair of shoes, or take a midday nap. You will only have time to focus on bettering your financial standing—*if* you are disciplined enough to do so.

Ambition | FOLLOW-UP ASSIGNMENT

1 Have you become complacent in the financial position you're in?

2 Have you ever felt jealous of the wealthy? Why or why not?

3   Do you find yourself procrastinating often? If so, why do you procrastinate?

4   What indulgences do you engage in that keep you from focusing on growth?

Wisdom

KNOWLEDGE IS POWERFUL....AND PROFITABLE.

"Poverty and shame shall be to him that refuseth instruction, but he that regardeth reproof shall be honored." ~Proverbs 13:18

Financial stability is not an accident. It's something you gain after learning (and doing) all the right things. Some things you will have to learn on your own through trial and error, but you would be foolish not to seek direction from those who have already accomplished what you want to accomplish. Some people are much too proud to seek guidance from anyone, but this puts limits on their potential. We can't make it but so far without guidance. The key is getting guidance from the right people— people who've already been where you are and made their way up the ladder. You can also learn what *not* to do from people who dropped the ball. Just be aware that at every step of the way, there will always be someone smarter and more experienced than you. If you keep learning, there will be no limits to your success.

MONEY CAN'T BUY HAPPINESS, BUT WISDOM CAN.

Happy is the man that findeth wisdom and the man that getteth an understanding. For the merchandise of it is better than the merchandise of silver, and the gain thereof than fine gold. She is more precious than rubies and all things thou can desire cannot be compared unto her. Length of her days is in her right hand, and in her left hand riches and honor." ~Proverbs 3:13-16

Money *can* buy happiness if your only problem in life is a lack of money. But we all know that money is seldom our only problem. We have relationship, health, spiritual, and mental challenges too. Money cannot possibly be the solution to *all* these things. Interestingly enough, Proverbs 3:13-16 says it is those who find *wisdom* and *understanding* who are happy, not necessarily those who have lots of money. It makes sense, because the thing that seems to disturb us the most is our inability to understand what's going on in our lives and the world at large.

The question "why" is always ringing through our minds. *"Why did this happen? Why did they do that to me? Why are things this way?"* We seek closure. But true closure can only be found in understanding. You may never know why something happened, and you may never get an apology, but if you have an *understanding* of what took place, then you will have closure. This is where your happiness will come from. Understanding makes it possible for us to find happiness in what has happened in the past, while wisdom makes it possible to create happiness for our future. With wisdom, we are able to make decisions that help prevent confusion and disaster from striking, thus leading us to a happier life. Money alone can never do this.

Wisdom | FOLLOW-UP ASSIGNMENT

1 When was the last time you read a financial book? What did you learn from it?

2 Who are you going to learn from to help you improve your finances?

3 What makes you happy?

4 Do you think you would be happier if you had more money? Why or why not?

Business Ethics

YOU MUST DO WHAT YOU NEVER DONE TO HAVE WHAT YOU NEVER HAD.

"Wealth gotten by vanity shall be diminished, but he that gathereth by labor shall be increased." ~Proverbs 13:11

Do you remember when old folks used to tell us to get an "honest job"? Well, they were on to something because God wants us to do that, too. Making money in fraudulent or deviant ways is not considered honest, but vain and self-serving. Usually, when people make money in these ways, they end up losing it somehow. And rightfully so. If you don't have the wisdom to make money in an honest way, you most likely don't have the wisdom to take care of the money either. You will likely waste it on luxuries or get yourself into situations that cause unnecessary debts and fees. So, what exactly is an honest job? Any job or business where you're providing a legitimate service for legitimate pay.

If you're a *business owner*, unreasonable prices can be considered dishonest because the customer will pay more than the product or service is worth. They'll most likely be disappointed with the service and may even spread bad reviews about your business. If you're an *employee*, being severely underpaid is an injustice too. Even though the job may be legitimate, it's dishonest on the part of your employer to pay such a low wage. Make it your goal to find an occupation that is likable, honest, and allows you to do your best work for fair pay. When we don't like what we do for work, we are capable of resorting to dishonest measures (such as cutting corners) to get the job done. It's a lot easier to do great work *and* build wealth when you're doing a job that you're passionate about. Not to mention, you will never feel guilty about the success you achieve when you know you achieved it honestly.

PRACTICE MAKES PERFECT.

"He becometh poor that dealeth with a slack hand, but the hand of the diligent maketh rich. He that gathereth in summer is a wise son, but he that sleepeth in harvest is a son that causeth shame." ~Proverbs 10:4-5

It isn't often that we do our best work when we're doing a job we dislike. Instead, we try to get it over with as soon as possible. And if we don't like the people we are working with, it makes it even worse. But we are to do our best work, even when we don't like what we're doing for a living. Doing your job sloppily may help you get the job done with little to no hassle, but it also causes you to lose opportunities for promotions and pay raises. These opportunities usually go to those who are outperforming others. The same applies if you're a business owner. If you want to have a competitive edge, you must strive to be one of the best in whatever field you work in. The only way to do that is to take time to master your craft. If you've already mastered it, keep improving your weak areas so that you will always stay ahead of the competition.

PUT YOUR MONEY WHERE YOUR MOUTH IS.

"In all labor there is profit, but the talk of the lips tendeth only to penury."
~Proverbs 14:23

We all have ideas of what we would like to accomplish in life. We enjoy daydreaming about it, writing it down, and talking about it. Talking, although it may come easy, still takes energy and brain power. We have to think about what we're going to say, express it in the most effective way, and then listen to, process, and respond to what the other person is saying back. Talking, on a small scale, *is* laborious. Because it gives us the feeling that we're laboring, it tricks our mind into thinking we've accomplished something simply by talking.

Maybe we've gotten a clearer idea of what we would like to do by expressing it out loud, but we do not truly get anything done unless we take *action*. But don't be intimidated by this because taking action doesn't mean that you are responsible for making everything happen on your own. You can definitely have others assist you along the way. In fact, you *should* have others assist you, especially if you're trying to accomplish something far more challenging than you care to do alone. Nevertheless, action must be taken, whether it be on your own or with someone else. Being stuck on merely thinking or talking about it is not going to lead you to prosperity.

OPEN FOR BUSINESS.

"He that withholdeth corn, the people shall curse him. But blessing shall be upon the head of him that selleth it. ~Proverbs 11:26

If you have an abundance of something that others lack or desire, would you keep it all to yourself or would you share some with the public? It would be nice if you made the resource or item accessible to them, but you don't have to make it accessible for free. Some will have you believe that the godly thing to do is to give it away free of charge, but Proverb 11:26 says you are *blessed* if you *sell* it. We must get comfortable with selling goods and services without feeling like we're doing some kind of injustice to the public by asking them to pay for what we have to offer. People who truly want what you're offering have no problem paying for it. Now, there will always be "cheap" people who want goods for free. They are the ones who will try to shame you for selling it, maybe even implying that you're taking advantage of others, or that your goods and services aren't worth the money. Don't let these people bully you into giving away or discounting your goods and services. If you feel like you want to donate or discount something, do it because you want to, not because someone made you feel like your goods weren't worth the asking price.

Business Ethics | FOLLOW-UP ASSIGNMENT

1 Do you like what you do for a living? Why or why not?

2 What skill would you like to master?

3 What dreams and goals do you have that you haven't acted upon yet? What are you waiting for?

4 Have you ever sold anything before? If so, did you enjoy it?

Tithes & Offerings

YOUR INPUT IS YOUR OUTCOME.

"Honor the Lord with thy substance and with the firstfruits of all thine increase. So shall thy barns be filled with plenty, and thy presses shall burst out with new wine." ~Proverbs 3:9-10

We know that God has an abundance of every resource we can ever think of. But when he blesses us with money, we are hesitant to give any of it away. The biggest complaint I've heard from believers in regard to giving is when they speak of tithing—giving 10% of your income to the church. I've always been perplexed by this because if you're regularly attending a church, and actually *learning* there, then it's odd not to give them a donation. After all, *the church* is giving to *you*. Not only are they feeding you the word of God, but they're also accommodating you with a building, light, heating/air, a place to sit, a restroom, and a kitchen with refreshments. These things cost money. The fact that some church members want to enjoy these things without making a contribution seems selfish, to say the least. Giving is supportive, but it also expresses our gratitude for what we have. If you're blessed, then you should want to share that blessing with someone so they can feel the same appreciation for God that you have.

Your firstfruits, as mentioned in *Proverbs 3:9-10,* should be given (or put aside) before you begin spending your "increase" on anything else. Notice that it says you should honor the Lord with *all* your increase. This is important to note because we don't always have an increase of money. Sometimes it's an increase of material items or non-tangible resources such as time or knowledge. These things can be tithed or offered as well. Some people find it difficult to donate or tithe on a regular basis because they don't always have *money* to give, but just because you don't have money doesn't mean you don't have *anything*. We always have something to give. If you find it most appropriate to give money, do it. Sometimes you may find that your time, words of wisdom, or emotional support may be more appropriate. Use your own discretion to decide what part of your increase you feel is appropriate to give. Just be sure that you are purposeful about *who* you choose to give to.

Tithes & Offerings | FOLLOW-UP ASSIGNMENT

1   How do you feel about tithing?

2   Do you enjoy giving?

3   Do you feel like you should give more often?

Saving

WHEN YOU SAVE FOR YOUR FUTURE, YOUR FUTURE IS SAFE.

"Go to the ant, thou sluggard. Consider her ways, and be wise. Which having no chief, overseer or ruler, provideth her bread in the summer, and gathereth her food in the harvest."~Proverbs 6:6-8

I'm currently building up my savings account, thanks to Proverbs 6:6-8. This scripture shows us the importance of saving by giving us an example of an ant that saves food for the seasons to come. I've decided that it's about time that I be as wise as the ant and do the same. Sometimes, when we have extra money, we're quick to spend it or give it away, but we don't prioritize saving it. I mean, let's face it: it feels better to treat ourselves to new things than to save the extra money. And technically, we should treat ourselves to a little fun when we get paid. No one wants to work all week but never be able to do anything enjoyable for themselves at the end of it. But we shouldn't overdo it to the point where we don't have anything left to save.

There are a couple of ways to save: You can have a set amount to save each week, such as $50 a week. Or you can save a percentage, like 15% a week. Choose whichever is best for you, but I would suggest that you choose the option that allows you to save the largest amount. After all, the goal isn't just to save, but to save enough to rely on in a time of need. You might've heard financial experts say "saving won't make you rich," but getting rich isn't the point of saving. Savings provides a safety net for emergencies and unexpected expenses.

If you haven't already, go ahead and begin building up a stable savings account. You can even have an emergency stash in your home. Storing it in a safe is the safest. (No pun intended.) Remember the scripture says the ant doesn't need an overseer to make her save for her future. As humans with more intelligence than an ant, we should save the way ants save without having someone make us do it. It would take discipline, but if an ant can be disciplined in this manner, so can we.

Saving | FOLLOW-UP ASSIGNMENT

1 How much do you have in your savings account right now? And are you happy with the amount?

2 If an emergency was to hit your household right now, would you be able to take care of it financially?

SHARING IS CARING.

"The rich ruleth over the poor and the borrower is a servant to the lender."
~Proverbs 22:7

If you've ever borrowed money or taken out a loan, you know this scripture to be true. Those who hold most of the power and resources in our country have very little empathy for people who are in less fortunate situations. They can be ruthless when it comes to pay wages, taxes, and prices. They take very little consideration of what people can truly afford. All they care about is the money they want to collect. The same goes for banks and loan companies. When they come to collect their money, they aren't concerned about what your other expenses might be. They just want their money, and they want it now.

It goes to show why we shouldn't borrow money unless we absolutely have no other option. If you must get a loan, have a pre-planned strategy for how you're going to pay the money back before you even borrow. Otherwise, you will be trapped in debt while having collectors bug you to pay up. And if you're unfortunate enough to owe the government, they will garnish your wages until the debt is paid. All of this will literally leave you feeling like a slave to the lender. But it proves how important it is to have our own money, because when we have to borrow someone else's, we always end up paying even more than we bargained for.

GIVE FREELY, BUT CAUTIOUSLY.

"Withhold not good from them to whom it is due when it is in the power of thine hand to do it. Say not unto thy neighbor, "Go and come again, and tomorrow I will give" when thou hast it by thee. ~Proverbs 3:27-28

From time to time, we run into people who need us to give them a loan of some kind. We don't always have the time, money, or materials to help them out, but when we do, we should. As we see in Proverbs 3:27-28, not only should we help them, we should do it as soon as possible. Stringing them along just because they're depending on you or creating unfair stipulations around your help is wrong. If you *can* help, do it. But always take precautions. Only lend to people you trust. They should be trustworthy enough to return an item in the same condition in which they received it. If it's money you loaned, they should return the full amount in the manner in which they received it, unless you agreed upon another method. If you feel it's safer to just donate the item or money without expecting a return or repayment, then that is fine. Some people feel like this method is easier because so many people seem to have a hard time paying back loans.

Loans wouldn't be so hard to pay back if people practiced the law of first fruits. Each payday, they would take out money off the top of their income, save it until they're done gathering all the money, then pay the loan back in full. This doesn't happen often because we aren't disciplined. Our bad money habits show why we need loans in the first place. Sometimes, the problem is not that we don't have enough money, but that we don't know how to *manage* money. We shouldn't have to repay someone in installments if they didn't loan it in installments. These are things *you* must consider before giving out a loan. But if you trust that the person has the means and responsibility to pay you back in full and on time, freely give them a hand.

YOU REAP WHAT YOU SOW.

"There is that scattereth, and yet increaseth, and there is that withholdeth more than is meet, but it tendeth to poverty. The liberal soul shall be made fat, and he that watereth shall be watered also himself." ~Proverbs 11:24-25

When we have a scarcity mindset, we think that if we give, we'll be the ones to go without. But there is a difference between giving and being taken from. What is *taken* from us is a loss, but what we *give* is a gain. How so, you say? Because God looks out for people who look out for the needy. He repays our generosity by being generous to us in return. Even when our resources are taken from us unjustly, he repays that too—if we're righteous. Take the story of Job, for instance. He was the most righteous man of his time, but he lost all his wealth when Satan took it from him. God restored it all, and then some. The story is a comforting read when you're dealing with loss, whether it be of money, materials, or the loss of a loved one (Job also lost his children). While Job grieved his loss, he continued to trust in God. The faith Job had is the faith we all should have while giving to the needy. Give from the heart, and trust that God will give you the proper repayment for your generosity. However, don't give just to get something in return. Your giving should be so genuine that you don't care if you receive a reward or not.

Loans | FOLLOW-UP ASSIGNMENT

1   Have you ever borrowed money before? What was that experience like for you?

2   Would you ever loan money to someone? Why or why not?

3   Do you give or donate anything to charity or those in need? Why or why not?

4   Do you think the world would be a better place if we were more giving? Why or why not?

Priorities

KEEP YOUR EYE ON THE PRIZE.

"He that tilleth, his hand shall be satisfied with bread. But he that followeth vain persons is void of understanding.~ Proverbs 12:11

Building wealth requires focus, but there are many distractions surrounding us that make it difficult for us to focus as we'd like to. Sometimes it's our own fault. We become busybodies, trying to find out what's going on in other people's lives. Staying updated with the latest celebrity gossip. Sharing news about the scandals going on with our neighbors. Comparing our lives to the influencers on social media. All of this might be entertaining, but it doesn't lead us to our own successes. It only makes us focus on the failures and successes of *other people's* lives instead. If you find yourself being distracted by others, then it's time to focus on your own life purpose. If you need help finding your purpose, there are people who can help you, such as life coaches and mentors. You can also read my book *Womanifest: A Girl's Guide to Spiritual Growth, Finding Purpose & Receiving Blessings* to help you. Whatever you do, remember that other people are living their own lives, and their lives have nothing to do with yours. Don't let it distract you from your own calling.

SHOW US WHAT YOU GOT.

"The slothful man roasteth not that which he took in hunting, but the substance of a diligent man is precious." ~Proverbs 12:27

Take a look at all that you've acquired over the course of your life. Physical assets and non-physical alike. Now ask yourself, *"What am I doing with what I have?"* We are always searching for new things, new ideas, and new opportunities to add to our lives, but there are already things, ideas, and opportunities that we have *now* that we should be using, but aren't. We know they have value of some kind, and we know we should use them at some point, yet we're still waiting on the perfect time to do so. The perfect time is now. Each and every day is a perfect time to make use of all your resources. Take inventory of everything you have that is just sitting there. Think of all the great ideas that you had that you never did anything about. Now, start brainstorming ways to make use of these things. You can't expect God to bless you with more if you aren't using what he's already given you.

 *Priorities* | FOLLOW-UP ASSIGNMENT

1   What is your biggest distraction?

2   What can you do to keep yourself from being distracted?

3   Are you maximizing the use of everything you have?

Humility

THE MEEK SHALL INHERIT THE EARTH.

"There is that maketh himself rich, yet has nothing. There is that maketh himself poor, yet hath great riches. ~Proverbs 13:7

We all know a few people who make themselves out to be way more than they are. They brag on themselves, talk about all the material things they have, and lead people to believe they have life all figured out. But 9 times out of 10, they're lying. These types are often the ones who lack the most peace and happiness in their lives, but attempt to cover it up with boasting. What's even sadder is that some people actually believe their lies. They believe they are as stable as they say they are, and they begin to aspire to be like them. Some may even get jealous of them. But it's all for nothing. The greatest people on earth are usually quiet, acting as if they are no better than anyone else. They are more humble than those who have accomplished a lot less, yet they are constantly bragging. Being humble is necessary to remain grateful for all that we have. Humility shows that we know God gave us abundance gracefully and lovingly. Not because we are inherently better or more deserving than others.

Humility | FOLLOW-UP ASSIGNMENT

1   Do you ever brag on yourself? Why or why not?

2   How do you feel about people who brag?

3   What are you most grateful for?

Future Planning

SLOW AND STEADY WINS THE RACE.

"Through wisdom is a house builded, and by understanding it is established, and by knowledge shall the chambers be filled with all precious and pleasant riches. ~Proverbs 24:3-4

The best thing you can do going forward is to continue to get educated about finances. Take your time to learn and apply the new knowledge, including what you learned in this book, little by little. As Proverbs 28:22 says, *"He that hasteth to be rich hath an evil eye and considereth not that poverty shall come upon him,"* don't be hasty and end up digging yourself into a financial hole. Wealth building is not a race. When you see others climbing the ladder, don't feel like you need to catch up to where they are, but definitely use their progress as motivation to achieve your own goals. Even if you aren't as far along on your journey as they are, simply knowing you're working on it will give you a boost of self-confidence. Lastly, always allow yourself to dream big. Limiting your dreams limits your success. As the saying goes, *"Shoot for the moon. If you miss, you'll land among the stars.* "It can never hurt to aim high, because failing will still put you in a comfortable spot.

IF YOU FAIL TO PLAN, YOU PLAN TO FAIL.

"A good man leaveth an inheritance to his children's children. And the wealth of the sinner is laid up for the just." ~ Proverbs 13:22

If nothing else motivates you to get financially stable, it should be the well-being of your family. There are way too many people in America living day to day with no plan for how they're going to take care of themselves in their latter days, nor do they know what they're going to leave to their offspring when they pass. While many view accumulating wealth as selfish, there *are* righteous reasons to do it, and leaving an inheritance is one of them. Proverbs 13:22 even tells us that the righteous will inherit the riches of the wicked. A great example of this would be those who do bad business. They mistreat their customers, offer substandard service or products, and then their customers end up leaving them and supporting the businesses of those that are honest and deliver quality service. The great thing about God's grace is that he not only blesses us with the wealth we worked for but also with what we earned by simply being good people. You should find it comforting that you don't have to labor for everything God has in store for you. He provides us with inheritances, just as we should provide our children with inheritances so they won't have to labor for everything they need in life.

Future Planning | FOLLOW-UP ASSIGNMENT

1   In the next 30 days, what are you going to do to improve your
    finances?

2   In the next 90 days, how much money do you plan to have in your
    bank account?

3   Do you plan to leave an inheritance for your offspring?

Righteousness

YOU CAN'T TAKE IT WITH YOU.

"Riches profit not in the day of wrath, but righteousness delivereth from death."
~Proverbs 11:4

Wealth can provide you with a comfortable lifestyle. It can even bring
popularity and privileges that most don't have, but what can it do for you
once you leave this earth? As Matthew 6:20 *"But lay up for yourselves
treasures in heaven where neither moth nor rust doth corrupt, and where
theives do not break in and steal."* It's good to have wealth on this side of
life, but we can't take it with us to the other side. The only thing that will
benefit us after death is how righteously we lived when we were alive.
Righteousness is the only ticket into the Kingdom. God is not taking cash
or credit.

Growing up as a Christian Baptist, I was led to believe that God and
money don't mix, but I was blown away by how many scriptures in the
book of Proverbs addressed wealth and poverty. For *Biblical Economics*, I
chose the scriptures that stood out to me the most, but there are many
others that weren't mentioned. I would encourage you to read the book

of Proverbs and see for yourself. The book is full of timeless wisdom on various topics. My goal for *Biblical Economics* is not necessarily to convince you to become wealthy, but to eradicate the scarcity mentality from your mind so that all successes are possible for you. Our view of money needs a major shift if we wish to be financially free.

I pray the clutches of financial instability is released off of you from this day forward. Gone are the days where you worked day in and day out without getting the pay you deserved. Gone are the days when you only have money to pay bills. Gone are the days when you could not treat yourself and your family to a well-deserved vacation. For now on, view money as a tool that makes your life (and others') easier. When we make money out to be more than a tool, that is when we end up loving it or being a slave to it. You do not have to love or hate money. But be grateful for it. Be grateful that you have it to advance yourself, take care of your family, and provide yourself with options and privileges that you couldn't enjoy while living paycheck to paycheck. Wishing you a lifetime of financial health. Thank you for supporting Queens of Virtue. God bless. ♥□

Queens of Virtue Marriage Prep & Femininity Coaching provides biblical based coaching to women of all ages on how to get in touch with their feminine nature. This service is mainly geared toward single women, as it is designed to help them prepare for marriage. However, many single *and* married women across the country and abroad have benefited from Queens of Virtue coaching, whether it was through one-on-one sessions, books, or free social media content. We have recently expanded our services to men as well. If you would like to request a coaching session or enroll in a course with Queens of Virtue, visit www.qovcoaching.com.